TECHNICAL
REPORT

Speaking with a Commonality Language

A Lexicon for System and Component Development

Bruce Newsome, Matthew W. Lewis, Thomas Held

Prepared for the United States Army

The research described in this report was sponsored by the United States Army under Contract No. W74V8H-06-C-0001.

ISBN: 978-0-8330-4180-7

The RAND Corporation is a nonprofit research organization providing objective analysis and effective solutions that address the challenges facing the public and private sectors around the world. RAND's publications do not necessarily reflect the opinions of its research clients and sponsors.

RAND® is a registered trademark.

Published 2007 by the RAND Corporation
1776 Main Street, P.O. Box 2138, Santa Monica, CA 90407-2138
1200 South Hayes Street, Arlington, VA 22202-5050
4570 Fifth Avenue, Suite 600, Pittsburgh, PA 15213-2665
RAND URL: http://www.rand.org/
To order RAND documents or to obtain additional information, contact
Distribution Services: Telephone: (310) 451-7002;
Fax: (310) 451-6915; Email: order@rand.org

Preface

In recent years, the U.S. Army has become increasingly interested in "commonality"—the sharing of common parts across different entities. Commonality has implications for procurers, designers, developers, trainers, logisticians, and operators. Unfortunately, commonality is poorly defined and conceptualized, which can contribute to confused discussion and poor decisionmaking. For example, engines are often described as "common," even if significant components, such as the turbocharger, have been removed to make the engines fit different vehicle types. This is not just a semantic challenge: An altered (uncommon) engine may increase costs if the extra development costs and failure risks are taken into account. A more rigorous lexicon can help delineate what is meant by a *common* or *uncommon* engine and thereby help decisionmakers determine the likely risks and rewards of each.

This report offers a new, more rigorous lexicon. It identifies nine terms that are often conflated with *commonality* and discretely defines and conceptualizes each using examples. This report complements other work, arising from the same project, which analyzes the consequences of commonality and how to optimally implement it. We hope that this report will serve as a sound basis for future reports, which would discuss in more detail how the new lexicon would improve decisionmaking and practice.

This research was sponsored by the Director of the Requirements Integration Directorate, Army Capabilities Integration Center, and was conducted within RAND Arroyo Center's Military Logistics Program. RAND Arroyo Center, part of the RAND Corporation, is a federally funded research and development center sponsored by the United States Army.

The Project Unique Identification Code (PUIC) for the project that produced this document is ATFCR06052.

For more information on RAND Arroyo Center, contact the Director of Operations (telephone 310-393-0411, extension 6419; FAX 310-451-6952; email Marcy_Agmon@rand.org), or visit Arroyo's Web site at http://www.rand.org/ard/.

Contents

Figures

Tables

Summary

In recent years, the Army, and the U.S. Department of Defense (DoD) more broadly, has become increasingly interested in "commonality"—the sharing of common parts across different entities. Commonality has implications for procurers, designers, developers, trainers, logisticians, and operators. Commonality offers many advantages and disadvantages; the trade-offs are sometimes difficult to discern and implement. To gain an understanding of the potential benefits and burdens (full life-cycle costs, training, and sustainment) of commonality, the U.S. Army Capabilities Integration Center asked RAND Arroyo Center to assess the consequences of "system and component commonality."[1]

Consequences are difficult to discern when there is confusion about the subject. As we began to examine existing literature on commonality, we realized that there is considerable confusion about what commonality is and why it matters. This report recommends a new, more rigorous lexicon for describing *system commonality* and *component commonality* and presents a common language for the Army and other services to share. This report provides definitions for *common* and eight related concepts.

We acknowledge that this work can be viewed as an unnecessary, pedantic exercise. However, the document was motivated both by the reported costs arising from a lack of clear definitions during recent Army acquisition processes and by cases in which unclear definitions of commonality have led to significant problems. This report documents historical examples of components being described as "common" and praised for their "interchangeability," even though they were neither perfectly common nor interchangeable. In fact, entities do not need to be common to be interchangeable. If two uncommon components mate with the same interface on a system and offer the same performance, they are perfectly interchangeable. Our definitions make these points clearer.

Definitions

In developing our lexicon, we examined current military and civilian use of the terms and sought, through our definitions, to clearly distinguish each term from the others and to resolve points of confusion surrounding the use of some of these terms.

---

[1] A follow-on document, *Assessing the Value of System and Component Commonality*, will address the consequences and effects of commonality more directly.

Common

Common items **are the same, for all intents and purposes, across more than one higher-level item.** We recommend this definition, in part, to distinguish common items from items that are not the same but that meet a standard or are interchangeable. Items do not need to be common to meet the same standards or to be interchangeable. For instance, two different brands of pneumatic tires might be interchangeable on certain vehicles because those tires meet the same relevant standards of size and pressure.

Standardized

We define *standardized* **as meeting a standard, such as a performance or material standard or a shared process or resource.** A *standard* is the measure specifying a level of performance (such as a component's stress threshold), material form (such as a component's size or interface), process (such as a vibration-mitigation process), or resource (such as 220-voltage electricity). *Standardization* is the process of establishing a standard. Items do not need to be common to meet the same standard, and vice versa.

Interchangeable

Interchangeable items **are defined as those capable of exchanging places without alteration.** This is an important distinction because, while all common items are interchangeable, not all interchangeable items are common.

Figure S.1 shows a Venn diagram of *common, standardized,* and *interchangeable,* as well as examples for each region of the figure.

Module

A *module* **can be defined as an exchangeable or augmentable item used to change the higher-level item's functionality.**[2] A *module* should be distinguished from an *interchangeable* item. While *interchangeability* refers to the exchange of items of the same type to replace a dysfunctional item, modules of *different* types are exchanged—or a module is added—to change an overall *system's* capabilities or attributes. Common modules can be interchanged if one fails, but dissimilar (not common) modules can also be interchanged to change the system's functionality.

Modular

A *modular item* **is one capable of changing functionality through the exchange or addition of modules.** A *modular item* should be distinguished from a *module* because these terms describe different levels (*system* and *component,* respectively).

Family

A *family* **is a set of functionally differentiated variants of a base model.**[3] Variants have something in common, though there is some uncertainty about how much or what they must share for them to share a base model.

---

[2] The word *exchangeable,* as it is used here, is distinct from *interchangeable.* Interchangeable items perform the same function, for all intents and purposes, whereas exchangeable modules offer new functions.

[3] We define a *base model* as a major item or collection of items shared, in practice or prospectively, across more than one higher-level item. A fuller discussion can be found in the section on "Family" in Chapter Three.

Figure S.1
Relationships Among Items That Are Interchangeable, Common, and Standardized, with Examples

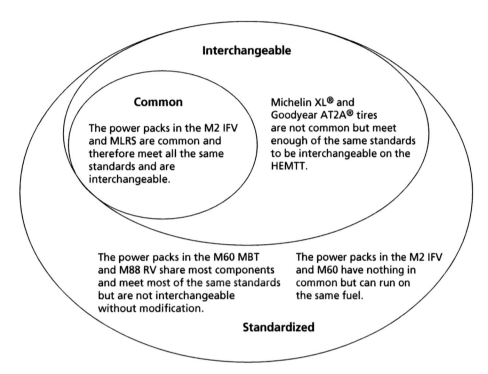

NOTE: HEMTT = heavy expanded mobile tactical truck; IFV = infantry fighting vehicle; MBT = main battle tank; MLRS = Multiple Launch Rocket System; RV = recovery vehicle.
RAND TR481-S.1

Hybrid

We define a *hybrid* as a combination of capabilities or components that are normally separated. The hybrid is important because it offers an alternative to modular items and family variants, in particular.

Interoperable

***Interoperable items* are able to work together; the ability to work together always has a context, which must be specified.** For instance, two weapons may be described as interoperable because they process the same targeting data. They are not necessarily common, nor do they necessarily share any components or standards.

Differentiated

***Differentiated* can be defined as having altered capabilities or items.** This definition is inherently comparative and contextual. These capabilities or items have been altered or are distinct from existing capabilities or items. *Differentiation* is an important concept, principally as a contrast to *common*. While common items are the same, differentiated items are in some way different or specialized ("stand-out" items) compared to other items or are stand-alone items.

Recommended Definitions

Table S.1 summarizes our recommended definitions. Although readers may not agree with all our definitions, we hope that this report will serve as a sound basis for a rigorous lexicon that the Army—at least its development, procurement, and logistics communities—could adopt and utilize for the better. Future work might address how this or another rigorous lexicon could improve decisionmaking across a broad spectrum of activities related to the acquisition and maintenance of Army systems. This report also complements other RAND work on the consequences of commonality.

Table S.1
Summary of Recommended Commonality-Related Definitions

Term	Definition
Common	Same across more than one higher-level item
Standardized	Meeting a standard, such as a performance or material standard or a shared process or resource
Interchangeable	Capable of exchanging places without alteration
Module	Exchangeable or augmentable item used to change the higher-level item's functionality
Modular	Capable of changing functionality through the exchange or addition of modules
Family	A set of functionally differentiated variants of a platform or base model
Hybrid	Having combined capabilities or items that are normally separate
Interoperable	Able to work together
Differentiated	Altered capabilities or items

Abbreviations

CFV	cavalry fighting vehicle
DoD	U.S. Department of Defense
HEMTT	heavy expanded mobile tactical truck
ICV	infantry carrier vehicle
IFV	infantry fighting vehicle
MBT	main battle tank
MLRS	Multiple Launch Rocket System
PUIC	Project Unique Identification Code
RV	recovery vehicle
SEP	Spitterskyddad Enhets Platform
SEV	specially equipped vehicle

CHAPTER ONE

Introduction

Increasingly, the U.S. Army, and the U.S. Department of Defense (DoD) more broadly, is emphasizing "commonality"—the sharing of common parts across different entities. Commonality has implications for procurers, designers, developers, trainers, logisticians, and operators.

Commonality offers advantages and disadvantages; the optimal trade-offs are sometimes difficult to discern and implement. On the plus side, commonality can increase operational and logistical flexibility. If the same component can be replaced on multiple systems,[1] the logistical burden decreases. Additionally, a common major component (such as a vehicle chassis) suggests common operational performance, helping different systems work together. Common major components are also expected to reduce development and procurement costs and permit the sharing of maintenance procedures and maintainers. However, commonality can decrease design freedom and operational flexibility by making components conform to different host systems and disallowing specialization. Moreover, the acquisition of common components across multiple systems might impose extra development or procurement burdens that outweigh the actual benefits. The Army needs to understand how commonality provides benefits and imposes new burdens and operational risks so that it can determine how much commonality should be sought. Therefore, the Army Capabilities Integration Center asked RAND Arroyo Center to assess the consequences of "system and component commonality."[2]

However, as we began to examine existing literature on commonality, we realized that there is considerable confusion about what *commonality* is and why it matters. The U.S. military's own definitions often overlap or contain inconsistencies. Worse, the U.S. military often fails to formally define some of the concepts that we have identified as relevant. This confusion leads to poor understanding of the benefits and burdens of commonality. For example, in 1994, the Committee on Appropriations of the U.S. House of Representatives suggested, with the President's approval, that DoD transfer some earth-orbiting satellites to an agency whose satellites, according to the manufacturer, had a significant proportion of components in "common" with the DoD satellites. Further study, however, revealed that most of those components were not interchangeable, though they did share a "common" development lineage. The contractor's earlier statements about common components had persuaded the government that integrating the two agencies' satellites would offer significant benefits. In fact, further study indicated that integration would not be beneficial to the government. Semantic impreci-

---

[1] According to our use here, the dividing line between the *component* and *system* categories is drawn by primary intended end use: If the item is intended to be functional alone, it is a *system*; otherwise, it is a *component*.

[2] A follow-on document, *Assessing the Value of System and Component Commonality*, will address the consequences and effects of commonality more directly.

sion had almost led the government to enact a disruptive policy that did not offer the benefits presumed. More rigorous agreement between the House of Representatives, the manufacturer, and DoD on the differences among terms such as *shared development lineage, common,* and *interchangeable* would have mitigated the confusion (Schultz, 1995).

This report recommends a new, more rigorous lexicon for describing commonality and presents a common language for the Army and its contractors and partners to share. Words matter: If we do not use words in the same way, we risk confusion and poor decisionmaking. Researchers can use rigorous definitions to help delineate problems and solutions and thus advance theory. Concept developers, procurers, and designers need such definitions to develop appropriate systems and components. Supply chain managers need such definitions to categorize and manage items. Trainers require definitions to help build a shared understanding within the learning community. Policymakers require clearly delineated concepts to support effective decisionmaking.

This report discusses *common* and eight related concepts that are often conflated with *commonality* but that we discretely define and conceptualize. For each concept, we provide examples of how these terms can be used in relation to vehicular and infantry weapons.[3] This report complements other RAND work on the consequences of commonality. Although the reader may not agree with all the definitions presented here, we hope that this report will serve as a sound basis for a future lexicon acceptable to the Army and for use in future reports that may discuss in more detail how the new lexicon would improve decisionmaking and practice.

The remainder of this report is organized as follows. Chapter Two develops a "system-component hierarchy" to help categorize *systems* and *components*. Chapter Three defines and conceptualizes *common* and eight other relevant terms. In Chapter Four, we present some examples of each of the nine concepts identified as relevant in this report. Chapter Five then offers some brief recommendations and conclusions.

---

[3] The examples in this document are mostly historical. More topical examples, such as from within the set of proposed equipment known as *future combat systems,* were not used because of the amount of uncertainty in their current development.

Systems and Components

RAND was asked to assess the consequences of "system and component commonality." This chapter explains the distinction between *systems* and *components*. Figure 2.1 shows the system-component hierarchy, which is illustrated in Figure 2.2 using the military example of the M4 carbine, an individual weapon issued to U.S. Army soldiers.

The dividing line between the component and system categories in Figure 2.1 is drawn according to primary intended end use—if the item is intended to be functional alone, it is a *system*; otherwise, it is a *component*. For example, the M4 carbine is a system because it is a final combination of products. However, a tank gun would be considered a component because it is designed to be installed on a tank.

Figure 2.1
System-Component Hierarchy

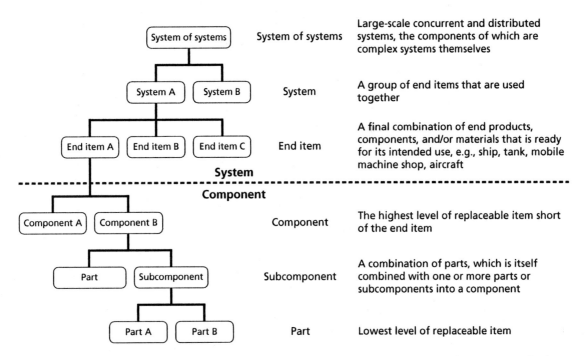

SOURCE: System of systems definition: Kotov (1997, p. 2); system, part definitions adapted from Joint Chiefs of Staff (2001); other definitions: Joint Chiefs of Staff (2001).
RAND TR481-2.1

Figure 2.2
The System-Component Hierarchy as Exemplified in the M4/M4A1 Carbine

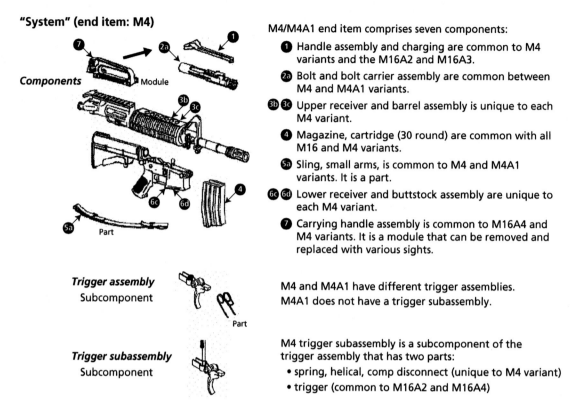

M4/M4A1 end item comprises seven components:

❶ Handle assembly and charging are common to M4 variants and the M16A2 and M16A3.

❷ⓐ Bolt and bolt carrier assembly are common between M4 and M4A1 variants.

❸ⓑ ❸ⓒ Upper receiver and barrel assembly is unique to each M4 variant.

❹ Magazine, cartridge (30 round) are common with all M16 and M4 variants.

❺ⓐ Sling, small arms, is common to M4 and M4A1 variants. It is a part.

❻ⓒ ❻ⓓ Lower receiver and buttstock assembly are unique to each M4 variant.

❼ Carrying handle assembly is common to M16A4 and M4 variants. It is a module that can be removed and replaced with various sights.

M4 and M4A1 have different trigger assemblies. M4A1 does not have a trigger subassembly.

M4 trigger subassembly is a subcomponent of the trigger assembly that has two parts:
• spring, helical, comp disconnect (unique to M4 variant)
• trigger (common to M16A2 and M16A4)

SOURCE: Headquarters, U.S. Department of the Army, U.S. Department of the Air Force, and U.S. Department of the Navy (2001).
RAND TR481-2.2

Our system-component hierarchy consists of six levels (part, subcomponent, component, end item, system, and system of systems), three within each category. The system category includes three levels: system of systems, system, and end item. The component category also has three levels: component, subcomponent, and part. Notice that this reduction leads to some semantic confusion. For instance, *a component* refers to one of the six levels, whereas *component* (according to our notation) refers to one of the two categories.

These categories and levels are drawn from existing military and civilian terms and definitions. They are not perfectly distinct—coding always will be subjective—but at least they give us a conceptual understanding of how the Army itself distinguishes between *systems* and *components*.

Beginning at the most micro level, notice that a part, such as the M4 carbine's sling, is the lowest level of *replaceable* item; it is not the lowest level of *manufactured* item—a part may be manufactured with multiple subpart items, such as the sling buckle, which are not replaced. Instead, only the part (the sling) is replaced.[1]

A subcomponent, of which the trigger assembly is an example, is a combination of parts that is itself combined with at least one other subcomponent or part to form a component. The subcomponent is neither the lowest level nor the highest level of replaceable item short

---

[1] The Defense Acquisition University (2005) does not define *part*.

of the end item. The component is the highest level of replaceable item short of the end item. Note that the subcomponent is not a necessary step between part and component—indeed, a component could be a part (such as the sling) if it is both the highest and lowest level of replaceable entity short of the end item. The end item, the M4 carbine itself, is a combination that is intended for stand-alone use. A system, such as a carbine carried on a vehicle as part of the latter's normal inventory, is a combination of end items.[2] A system of systems, such as a unit deploying vehicles both with carbines and machine guns and with infantry squads, is a combination of systems.

The M-4 carbine in Figure 2.2 is an *end item*: It is a final assembly of components that is ready for its intended use. As an end item, it falls within the *system* category of our system-component categorization.

According to its manual,[3] the M4 carbine is composed of seven *components*. One component (the sling) is also a *part*, since it is the lowest level of replaceable item (even though it is manufactured from other items, such as the canvas strip and the buckle). The other six components are not parts, since they are not the lowest level of replaceable item. Instead, these six components are composed of subcomponents and parts. For instance, the trigger assembly is a subcomponent of the lower receiver and buttstock assembly. The trigger subassembly is a subcomponent within the trigger assembly. The trigger subassembly is composed of two parts, the spring and the trigger.

The next chapter defines the nine relevant concepts identified in this report.

---

[2] The Defense Acquisition University (2005, p. B-55) defines *end item* as "[t]he final production product when assembled, or completed, and ready for issue or deployment." Our definition of *end item* seeks to accommodate the implicit hierarchical difference between a system and other forms of product. The Defense Acquisition University (p. B-159) defines *system* as a "combination of two or more interrelated pieces of equipment (or sets) arranged in a functional package to perform an operational function or to satisfy a requirement." (This definition is the second of two; the first refers to *organization*.) We observe too much overlap in these two definitions and prefer to make explicit the hierarchical relationship between *end item* and *system*.

[3] Headquarters, U.S. Department of the Army, U.S. Department of the Air Force, and U.S. Department of the Navy (2001).

CHAPTER THREE

Commonality-Related Concepts and Definitions

This chapter defines and conceptualizes *commonality* and its related concepts. Nine main concepts are identified in this document as relevant to *commonality*. Most can be categorized as mostly characteristic of either the component or system category or, in the case of *differentiated*, both:

- component category: common, standardized, interchangeable, module
- system category: modular, hybrid, family, interoperable
- both categories: differentiated.

The remainder of this chapter discusses existing definitions of each of these nine concepts (see Table 3.1) and provides our recommended definitions. These recommended definitions are summarized in Table 3.2.

Common

Commonality is the key concept in this report. However, as we illustrate here, because this term is so widely used and can have so many different meanings, its appropriate meaning within the procurement and development communities is difficult to ascertain. For instance, *common* can be used as a synonym for *ubiquitous, available, cheap,* or *similar*; however, not all of these meanings (e.g., *ubiquitous*) are useful in helping developers or procurers determine what sort of components or systems are needed. A basic objective of this report is to provide the Army with a definition of *common* as well as a range of related terms that will allow for more precise and focused procurement and development discussions. *Commonality* is a widely used term with many meanings, not all of which are useful for the procurement or development communities. Our recommendations do not imply that the many meanings of *common* can be eliminated. Rather, we recommend that the procurement and development communities, in particular, use our narrower definition.

The *Department of Defense Dictionary of Military and Associated Terms* (Joint Chiefs of Staff, 2001, p. 105) does not define *common*, but it does define *common item*, a term with a wide range of meanings:

> 1. Any item of materiel that is required for use by more than one activity. 2. Sometimes loosely used to denote any consumable item except repair parts or other technical items. 3. Any item of materiel that is procured for, owned by (Service stock), or used by any Military Department of the Department of Defense and is also required to be furnished to a

Table 3.1
Existing Definitions of the Nine Commonality-Related Concepts

Concept	DoD or Army Definition	Problems with Definition	Synonyms and Related Terms	Typical Context
Common	"[L]ike and interchangeable characteristics," "components," or "consumable items"[a]	Conflated with *interchangeable*	Uniform[b]	Components
Standardized	"Cooperation" and common "procedures," "doctrine," or components[a]	Conflated with *interchangeable* and *interoperable*	Rationalized, ubiquitous, generic, approved	Components, munitions, fuel, training, performance
Interchangeable	Subsumed by DoD definition of *common*	Conflated with *common*	Substitutable	Components, munitions
Module	(1) Unit of measurement, (2) building unit, (3) software, component[c]	Examples, not a definition	See synonyms for *modular*	Subsystems
Modular	*Modular design* is defined as "[a] modular building block principle which ordinarily employs quick disconnect technique features."[c]	Wordy	Composite,[d] compartmentalized, adaptable	Software, electronics, vehicles
Family	A *family of systems* is defined as "independent systems that can be interconnected or related in various ways to provide different capabilities."[e]	Definition of *system* too broad	Derivatives, upgrades, modifications	Components, processes, knowledge, personnel
Hybrid	None	NA	Multirole, multipurpose, general-purpose, universal, versatile	Multirole aircraft, IFVs
Interoperable	Compatible "communications-electronics systems" or "equipment"[a]	Excludes compatible performance	Jointness, international standardization,[f] compatible	Coalition, services, branches, IT
Differentiated	None	NA	Specialized, stand-alone, hived off[g]	MBTs, fighters, bombers

NOTE: NA = not applicable. MBT = main battle tank. IFV = infantry fighting vehicle.
[a] Joint Chiefs of Staff (2001).
[b] Smith (1987, p. 92).
[c] Headquarters, U.S. Department of the Army (1983).
[d] Meyer and Lehnerd (1997, p. 83).
[e] Office of the Under Secretary of Defense for Acquisition, Technology, and Logistics (undated).
[f] Simpkin (1979, p. 206) and Merriman (1987, p. 92).
[g] Simpkin (1979, p. 177).

Table 3.2
Recommended Definitions of the Nine Commonality-Related Concepts

Term	Definition
Common	Same across more than one higher-level item
Standardized	Meeting a standard, such as a performance or material standard or a shared process or resource
Interchangeable	Capable of exchanging places without alteration
Module	Exchangeable or augmentable item used to change the higher-level item's functionality
Modular	Capable of changing functionality through the exchange or addition of modules
Family	A set of functionally differentiated variants of a platform or base model
Hybrid	Having combined capabilities or items that are normally separate
Interoperable	Able to work together
Differentiated	Altered capabilities or items

recipient country under the grant-aid Military Assistance Program. 4. Readily available commercial items. 5. Items used by two or more Military Services of similar manufacture or fabrication that may vary between the Services as to color or shape (as vehicles or clothing). 6. Any part or component that is required in the assembly of two or more complete end-items.

The DoD definition is so broad that almost any item might be classified as a common item. Meanwhile, the definition does not specifically include the least ambiguous use of the term *common item*—an item that is the same across more than one type of higher-level item. This last definition is closest to those found in the civilian literature on manufacturing, some of which we quote here to document the diversity of definitions and conceptualization. For example, in a study of civilian design, Perera, Nagarur, and Tabucanon (1999, p. 110) define *component commonality* as "the situation in which several components are replaced by a single component that can perform the functions of all of them." Eynan and Rosenblatt (1996, p. 93) define *component commonality* as "the replacement of several different components (subassemblies) by one component (subassembly)." Nagarur and Azeem (1999, p. 125) define *common components* as components that "replace unique components in several final products." These civilian definitions refer to multiple components replaced by a single component and imply an objective. The enabling factor is the use of a common component: The same item can be used in different systems to perform the same function. Common items are completely interchangeable among systems because they are the same component. However, not all interchangeable items are common.

The DoD (Joint Chiefs of Staff, 2001, p. 104) definition of *commonality* conflates *common* and *interchangeable*:

A quality that applies to materiel or systems: a. possessing like and interchangeable characteristics enabling each to be utilized, or operated and maintained, by personnel trained on the others without additional specialized training; b. having interchangeable repair parts and/or components; and c. applying to consumable items interchangeably equivalent without adjustment.

We find the conflation of *common* and *interchangeable* to be problematic. If *common items* are the same across more than one system, they are also interchangeable across those systems. However, interchangeable items are not necessarily common. For instance, different kinds of tires made by different manufacturers could be interchanged on one automobile, as long as the tires meet some of the same standards (e.g., diameter, among other attributes), as defined by the user.[1] Simpkin (1979, p. 67) distinguishes *commonality* from interchangeability in the context of weapons,[2] reasoning that guns might be assembled in different mountings for different weapon platforms. The gun tubes might remain common, but the gun assemblies would not, because they could not be exchanged without alteration. On the other hand, two uncommon gun assemblies, even with uncommon gun tubes, might be interchangeable if the gun assemblies mated with the same interface on two different platforms. Often, many different types of machine guns can be attached to the simple machine-gun mounts atop military vehicles.

Similarly, we also conclude that the use of *common* to refer to *uniform* is overinclusive and lacks the precision needed in the procurement and development context. The notion of *uniformity* can include nonmaterial factors, as described by Smith (1987, p. 20), who defined it as follows:

> Something more than the mechanical ability to produce things with standardized or interchangeable parts. It also refers to a pervasive mental attitude common among soldiers and essential to military enterprise that emphasizes system and order in all things, including labor on and off the shop floor.

We conclude that a narrower and more focused definition of *common* will be most useful for describing components. We recommend the following definition of *common components*: items that are the same, for all intents and purposes, across more than one higher-level item. We recommend this definition, in part, to distinguish common items from components that are not the same but that meet a standard (i.e., standardized items) or that are not the same but are interchangeable.

Standardized

Like *common*, the word *standard* (see Table 3.1), as it is currently used, takes on a number of different meanings, ranging, in this case, from *ubiquitous* or *generic* (as in the phrase, "the Army's standard wheeled vehicle") to *approved* (as in the phrase, "the Army's standard weapon training"). In the context of weapons, Simpkin (1979, p. 206) and Merriman (1987, p. 92) both use "international standardization" to mean international interoperability. The multiple

---

[1]   The user might distinguish between physical and functional interchangeability. Physical interchangeability refers to the ability to interchange items, at least because they fit the same interfaces, even if those items do not offer the same functionality. For example, one gun might be physically interchanged for another, even though the second gun does not fire the same ammunition. Functional interchangeability is a more demanding requirement, since the replacement must offer the same functionality, as defined by the user, as the replaced item.

[2]   Elsewhere, Simpkin (1979, p. 212) used both "standardization" and "inter-changeability" to describe components.

definitions of *standardized* and the term's confusion with other concepts, such as *common* or *interchangeable*, suggest that a more focused definition is needed.

Standardized is a term that is often used interchangeably with *common*. For instance, Perera, Nagarur, and Tabucanon (1999, p. 110) treat component standardization and component commonality as the same thing. Meanwhile, Ogorkiewicz (1970, p. 136), writing on armored fighting vehicles, defines *standardization* as "concentration on a minimum number of types of equipment." *Rationalization* is usually used to describe a similar process of reducing the number of components. One way to standardize or rationalize in this sense is to replace some different types of items with a common item.

DoD (Joint Chiefs of Staff, 2001, p. 506) defines *standardization* in terms of commonality, interchangeability, and interoperability:

> The process by which the Department of Defense achieves the closest practicable co-operation among the Services and Defense agencies for the most efficient use of research, development, and production resources, and agrees to adopt on the broadest possible basis the use of: a. common or compatible operational, administrative, and logistic procedures; b. common or compatible technical procedures and criteria; c. common, compatible, or interchangeable supplies, components, weapons, or equipment; and d. common or compatible tactical doctrine with corresponding organizational compatibility.

We define *standardized* as meeting a standard, such as a performance or material standard or a shared process or resource (see Table 3.2). A *standard* is the measure specifying a level of performance (such as a component's stress threshold), material form (such as a component's size or interface), process (such as a vibration-mitigation process), or resource (such as 220-voltage electricity). *Standardization* is the process of establishing a standard. Items do not need to be common to meet the same standard, and vice versa.

Unlike common items, standardized items come together for a common purpose (shared processes or resources) and must meet certain criteria (standards), but are not identical to each other. Systems, not just components, can be described as standardized if they share processes or resources or meet the same standards. For example, guns may fire common ammunition, and vehicles may run on common fuel. Here, care is taken to distinguish between the common resource (ammunition or fuel) and the standardized system (the guns or vehicles, respectively). Also, it is worth remarking that the use of the word *standardized* here, as with all the terms defined in this report, is highly contextual. The guns are standardized to common ammunition and the vehicles are standardized to common fuel, but they may share no other standards.

Interchangeable

Interchangeable and *interchangeability* are not officially defined by the DoD or Army dictionaries (see Table 3.1). Instead, the DoD dictionary conflates *interchangeability* and *commonality* in its definition of *common item*. We distinguish the two.[3]

---

[3] The Defense Acquisition University (2005, p. B-84) defines *interchangeability* as a "condition that exists when two or more items possess such functional and physical characteristics as to be equivalent in performance and durability, are capable of being exchanged one for the other without alteration on the items themselves or of adjoining items, except for adjustment, and without selection for fit and performance."

Following Simpkin's (1979, p. 67) analysis of tank design, we define *interchangeable items* as those that are capable of exchanging places *without alteration*. There is an important distinction to be noted between *interchangeable* items and *standardized* ones, since the latter must be adapted to work with different higher-level items. The need for alterations increases with more complex items. Simpkin, for instance, noted that engines and armaments are often altered to fit into different weapon platforms. Even if not altered themselves, these components may be fitted into different mountings. For example, a gun will usually require unique mountings on different tank models.

The British L7 105-mm tank gun illustrates the importance of this distinction. During the 1960s and 1970s, this gun became the most widely procured tank gun internationally, and, even today, it remains a popular choice for lighter armored vehicles.[4] As a result, different tanks were often described as carrying a "common" or "standardized" L7 tank gun. However, we find the use of these two terms imprecise in this context. Few of these different types of vehicles could exchange guns without extensive modification. For instance, a version of the L7 with a rotated breech was fitted onto Saudi T55 tanks to better fit the configuration of Soviet tanks. "Light-recoil" versions of the L7 have been fitted onto light armored vehicles, such as wheeled armored cars. Finally, the L7 mounted on the S-tank was a lengthened version. Adapted guns remain attractive because they are usually cheaper to procure than newly designed guns, and they are usually able to fire common ammunition. However, we must be semantically clear: A redesigned gun is not common with its parent. For example, the parent of a light-recoil variant does not perform to the same recoil standard as its variant.

The most frequent context for interchangeability is in reference to ammunition, though ammunition interchangeability is usually termed *standardization* or *commonality*, terms that are less precise in this context, as the case of the L7 illustrates. Decker (1999, p. 319) characterizes "standardized" NATO 120-mm tank ammunition as "one of the largest contributors to the logistical support of tank warfare." Ammunition is not normally considered a component, but certain ammunition nevertheless can be described as *common*, *standard*, or *interchangeable*. In the case of NATO 120-mm tank ammunition, if produced to the same design, the ammunition is better described as common than as standardized. Different guns that use it would be standardized to the common ammunition.

In summary, we recommend (see Table 3.2) that "interchangeable" items be defined as those "capable of exchanging places without alteration." This is an important distinction because, while all common items are interchangeable, not all interchangeable items are common. Figure 3.1 shows a Venn diagram of *common*, *standardized*, and *interchangeable*, along with examples for each region of the figure.

---

[4] Considering fully tracked tanks alone, the L7 was mounted on the British Centurion Mark V (first deployed in 1959); the Vickers Vijayanya (built for India); the U.S. M60 (first delivered in 1962) and M60A1; the German Leopard 1 (1965); the Swedish (turretless) Stridsvagn 103, or S-tank (1966); the Japanese Type 74 (1975); the Israeli Merkava I (1979) and II; the M1 Abrams (1980); the South Korean XM1; the Argentinean TAM; Spanish and Israeli M47 and M48 Patton tanks; and Saudi and Israeli T55 tanks.

Figure 3.1
Relationships Among Items That Are Interchangeable, Common, and Standardized, with Examples

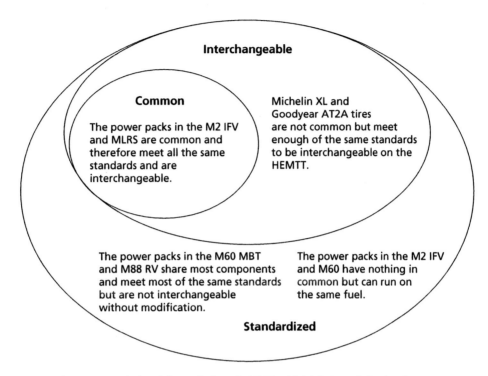

NOTE: HEMTT = heavy expanded mobile tactical truck; MLRS = Multiple Launch Rocket System; RV = recovery vehicle.
RAND TR481-3.1

Module

The *Department of Defense Dictionary of Military and Associated Terms* (Joint Chiefs of Staff, 2001) does not define *module* or any semantic derivatives, such as *modularity* or *modular* (see Table 3.1). The U.S. Army dictionary does provide several definitions of *module*, which apply in different contexts:

A standard or unit for measuring.

In building, a selected unit of measure, ranging in size from a few inches to several feet, used as a basis for planning and standardization of building materials.

In automatic data processing, a program unit that is discrete and identifiable with respect to compiling, combining with other units and unloading; e.g., the input from an assembler.

An item, assembly, subassembly, board, card, or component which is designed as a single unit to facilitate and simplify production line techniques, transportation, supply, and maintenance processing. (Headquarters, U.S. Department of the Army, U.S. Department of the Air Force, and U.S. Department of the Navy, 2001)

Different civilian communities have also put forth a number of definitions of the word *module*, including the following, which apply in different contexts:

> 4. *Electronics* A self-contained assembly of electronic components and circuitry, such as a stage in a computer, that is installed as a unit. 5. *Computer Science* A portion of a program that carries out a specific function and may be used alone or combined with other modules of the same program. 6. [*Aerospace*] A self-contained unit of a spacecraft that performs a specific task or class of tasks in support of the major function of the craft. (*American Heritage Dictionary of the English Language*, 2000)

The main difference between civilian and military use of the term *module* relates to the stage in a system's use and life cycle at which modules are reconfigured. The military is typically concerned with rapid reconfiguration of systems in the field through the addition or exchange of modules by users who intend to tailor equipment to different mission requirements. A long-standing example of a module used to augment an infantry weapon is an optical sight, which replaces "iron" or "vane" sights. An image-intensifying sight could be fitted for nighttime operations, while a normal optical sight could be fitted for daytime operations.

In contrast, civilian modules are typically reconfigured during design, development, and manufacture. Baldwin and Clark (2000, p. 63) note that "modules are units that are structurally independent of one another, but work together" according to "a predetermined set of design rules" (p. 6). Baldwin and Clark (2000) and Meyer and Lehnerd (1997) use the word *interface* to describe how components interact.[5]

Baldwin and Clark (2000) define *modularity* as "a nested hierarchical structure of interrelationships among the primary elements of the set" (p. 11), or "a particular design structure, in which parameters or tasks are interdependent within units (modules) and independent across them" (p. 88).

Baldwin and Clark's conceptualization of modularity is focused on the designer's and manufacturer's manipulation of modules to meet new market or client requirements. (Changing a product to make it more marketable is often termed *differentiation*, which is discussed later in this report.) Baldwin and Clark (2000, pp. 123–138, 227–228, 262) conceptualize several design processes that are expected to differentiate a product. "Substituting one module for another" could be used to augment the higher-level item or to lower costs. "Augmenting" an item by "adding a new module to the system" adds capabilities or improves performance, rather than simplifying the design or lowering costs. "Excluding" a module from the higher-level item would be expected to lower costs, possibly at the expense of performance or capabilities, and could still result in differentiation by refining the item's specialty. Indeed, Baldwin and Clark (2000, pp. 137, 301–310) note the virtue of an "exclude-then-augment" design strategy, which allows very narrow specialization at low cost by initially excluding extra

---

[5] Baldwin and Clark (2000, p. 64) use the word *interface* to describe how a module or any other "element interacts with the larger system." "An interface is a preestablished way to resolve potential conflicts between interacting parts of a design" (p. 73). Meyer and Lehnerd (1997, pp. 180–181) categorize interfaces in three ways: "1. the platform's subsystems interact within the platform, such as the ways in which the engine of an automobile interacts with a transmission; 2. the platform interacts with the user or other exogenous systems, such as the ways in which a user inputs information into a personal computer using a keyboard or mouse; 3. the platform interacts with add-on modules, such as the ways in which an internet browser's software interacts with plug-in applications for translating content originally downloaded in a foreign language."

modules, with room for augmentation later. Baldwin and Clark (pp. 140–142, 339) use the word *porting* to describe the assignment of a module from one product to another.

For the Army's purposes, we recommend a definition of a module as an exchangeable or augmentable item used to change the higher-level item's functionality (see Table 3.2). A module should be distinguished from an interchangeable item. Modules of different types are exchanged—or a module is added—to change the higher-level item's capabilities or attributes. *Interchangeability* refers to the exchange of items of the same type, including across different systems, usually made to replace a dysfunctional component but not to change the higher-level item's functionality.[6] Modules of different types can be exchanged because they fit the same interface. An augmenting module is added without replacing anything. For instance, some infantry weapons can mount an optical sight without removing the iron or vane sight.

Modular

DoD does not provide an official definition of the term *modular* (see Table 3.1). The U.S. Army dictionary defines *modular design* as a "modular building block principal which normally employs quick disconnect technique features and is the method used by materiel developers to simplify design and construction, or assembly, and to optimize on a means for fault isolation/diagnosis, replacement, and repair of those modules which malfunction or become defective." (Headquarters, U.S. Department of the Army, 1983, p. 121). This definition does not refer to a change in functionality, which, as pointed out in the discussion of modules, is a necessary outcome if an item is to be considered a module.

Thus, we recommend the following definition of *modular item*: a higher-level item capable of changing functionality through the exchange or addition of modules. A modular item should be distinguished from a module because these terms describe different levels of the system-component hierarchy. For instance, a rifle that can fit a number of different types of optical sight is a modular system, whereas the optical sights are modules.

Family

Although not defined in the DoD dictionary (Joint Chiefs of Staff, 2001; see also Table 3.1), the word *family* is commonly used in military science to refer to a set of items based on a "base model" or "platform," such as a vehicle chassis. (Since, in military usage, the word *platform* usually refers to a vehicle, we prefer the term *base model* to describe the common basis for a family of variants.)

In management science, a family is a set of products with something in common. For Meyer and Lehnerd (1997, pp. xi, 35), writing in the context of electronic products, a family is a set of "individual products that share common technology and address related market applications." They refer to a "common core technology" or "product platform," which they define as "a set of common components, modules, or parts from which a stream of derivative products can be efficiently created and launched" (p. 7) or "a set of subsystems [components] and

---

[6] This case parallels the interchange of an identical module as an interchangeable part to achieve the original functionality.

interfaces that form a common structure from which a stream of derivative products can be efficiently developed and produced" (pp. xii, 39). Meyer and Lehnerd's definition of *families* in terms of "subsystems" and "interfaces" overlaps with Baldwin and Clark's definition of *modularity*. For Meyer and Lehnerd, subsystems are discrete items that have a "specific function" or that can be produced in isolation from the other items before being installed into the base model itself (p. 39). Baldwin and Clark (2000, p. 63) prefer to call these subsystems *modules*.

We think that the term *family* can be defined much more cleanly and simply as a set of items sharing a base model.

Coding a Base Model

There is considerable uncertainty about the circumstances under which a set of common components actually constitutes a base model. Standardizing or selecting common components across items does not necessarily create a base model. For example, we would not consider two models of wheeled vehicles to share a base model just because they share the same type of wheel. Robertson and Ulrich (1998), writing in the context of the automobile industry, define a base model as "the collection of assets shared by a set of products."[7] For Robertson and Ulrich, the *proportion* of shared components must cross some threshold to establish a base model (p. 20). They imply that the threshold should be "most" (more than 50 percent) components:

> Generally, platform products [variants] share many if not most development and production assets. In contrast, parts-standardization efforts across products may lead to the sharing of a modest set of components, but such a collection of shared components is generally not considered a product platform [base model]. (p. 20)

Meyer and Lehnerd (1997, p. 120) agree that sharing a few or minor components is not enough to create a base model. They assert that products must share major "subsystems" and "interfaces" if they are to share a base model (p. 39). For instance, an automobile base model includes at least a chassis, engine, drive train, and transmission. Ultimately, the composition of the base model is left to the producers. "Every company must determine precisely the structure of the product platforms [base models] suitable for its business" (p. 39). Meyer and Lehnerd (pp. 30, 42–43) also allow that a base model can be modified without declaring a new base model. A "platform [base model] extension occurs when particular subsystems within the existing platform [base model] design are substantially changed and enhanced." A new base model occurs when new subsystems are added or the old subsystems are combined in a new way, rather than just changed internally. Despite these coding rules, the coding remains subjective. We define a *base model* as a major item or collection of items shared, in practice or prospectively, across more than one higher-level item.

---

[7] Robertson and Ulrich (p. 20) divide "assets" into four categories: (1) components, "the part designs of a product, the fixtures and tools needed to make them, the circuit designs, and the programs burned into programmable chips or stored on disks"; (2) processes, "the equipment used to make components or to assemble components into products and the design of the associated production process and supply chain"; (3) knowledge, "design know-how, technology applications and limitations, production techniques, mathematical models, and testing methods"; and (4) people and relationships, "teams, relationships among team members, relationships between the team and the larger organization, and relationships with a network of suppliers."

Variants

Meyer and Lehnerd (1997) refer to products within the family as *derivatives*, which are often termed *variants* in the military context. Families of military items consist of a set of functionally differentiated variants. Most weapon platforms have been designed to serve one function. Modified or upgraded equipment will share many components with the equipment's parent but do not change the original function and are therefore probably not best described as *variants*. Some derivatives (for example, command, mortar-carrier, ambulance, and training variants of a light armored vehicle) are certainly variants but may be considered unremarkable because they do not differ sufficiently from the parent. To capture unremarkable variants, Terry et al. (1991, p. 164) distinguished between a *variant* and a "specially equipped vehicle" (SEV), such as the M113 ambulance. "An SEV is a standard vehicle, such as the [U.S. M113] infantry section carrier, which is fitted with a kit to allow it to perform a special function." The kit does not change the basic structure. For Terry et al., an example of a vehicle variant is the M577 command post vehicle, adapted from the M113 armored personnel carrier. The body of the M577 is taller than that of the M113. For Terry et al., this difference means that the two vehicles have different chassis (even though the running gear is the same). "A variant is a vehicle whose characteristics are so different from those of the basic vehicle on which its design is based that the chassis is itself different" (p. 164). The level of "difference" is a subjective coding problem and not one that Terry et al. investigate further.

We conclude that *variants* are functionally differentiated derivatives of a base model (see Table 3.2). Like base models, variants face a coding problem, which is inherently subjective and otherwise beyond our purposes here.

In summary, a *family* is a set of functionally differentiated variants of a base model. Variants have something in common, though there is some uncertainty about how much or what they must share to also share a common base model.

Hybrid

Although used frequently in biology and management science, the terms *hybridization* and *hybrid* are not common in military science; neither is defined by DoD (see Table 3.1). *Hybridization* is used here to mean the process of combining multiple items or capabilities that are normally separated. We define *hybrid* as an item combining capabilities or lower-level items that are normally separated.

In military science, hybrids tend to be described by terms such as *universal, multirole, multipurpose,* and *versatile. Universal* was once a popular term for describing multifunctional items.[8] Today, the most frequently used terms for military hybrids include *versatile, multipurpose,* and *multirole.* Many authors describe armored vehicles and aircraft as *multirole* or *multipurpose* if they perform more than one of the functions normally assigned to discrete weapons (see Simpkin, 1979, pp. 189–196; and Walker, 1987, p. 2). For instance, aircraft capable of,

---

[8] For instance, just before World War II, the British Army introduced a "universal carrier" (a small, armored, tracked vehicle) to replace the armored carriers used to transport the infantry's heavy weapons and ammunition. In 1943, the British aircraft manufacturer Hawker produced a "universal" wing for the fourth "mark" of the Hurricane aircraft. The universal wing could be mounted with any of the weapons that previously required specialized wings; thus, the new wing, with its hybrid capabilities, replaced all the previous wings (Winchester, 2004, p. 117). In 1945, the British used the word *universal* to define a class of tanks replacing the infantry and cruiser tank classes.

or tasked with, air-superiority or -interception missions as well as ground-attack missions are often described as *multirole aircraft*.

We prefer the clear and multidisciplinary meaning of the word *hybrid* (see Table 3.2). We define a *hybrid* as a combination of capabilities or items that are normally separated. For example, an IFV combines external armaments with personnel carrying capabilities.[9] The concept of the *hybrid* is important because it offers an alternative to modular items and family variants, in particular.

Interoperable

Interoperability means that items are able to work together. DoD treats interoperability more parochially—as compatible services or information technology (see Table 3.1):

> 1. The ability to operate in synergy in the execution of assigned tasks. 2. The condition achieved among communications-electronics systems or items of communications-electronics equipment when information or services can be exchanged directly and satisfactorily between them and/or their users. The degree of interoperability should be defined when referring to specific cases. (Joint Chiefs of Staff, 2001, p. 275)

While the ability to communicate is an important test of interoperability, it is not the only test. Shared mobility is a neglected type of interoperability. For instance, bomber aircraft may be vulnerable to enemy fighter planes if friendly fighter escorts cannot operate at similar ranges. Similarly, vehicles in ground units are expected to operate with similar speed, refueling range, target engagement range, and mobility.

The ability to work together must be contextual: Interoperability can be assessed in one context without implying interoperability in other contexts. For example, two weapons could be interoperable in terms of range (perhaps they can engage targets accurately at the same distance or travel the same distance without refueling) but not speed (one is slower than the other). In the end, interoperability offers a subjective coding problem, like *base model* and *variant*, that our definition is not intended to solve.

Some forms of interoperability are even less obvious and more difficult to measure. For instance, tanks produced with Chobham or equivalent armor[10] are interoperable in the sense that similarly protected tanks can withstand similar threats and carry out or support similar missions. This form of interoperability is limited to force employment and has no logistical consequences (Terry et al., 1991, p. 20).

As noted earlier in this chapter, Simpkin (1979, p. 206) treats "international standardization" as a synonym for *interoperability* in the context of land weapons. The U.S. Army is rightly concerned with interoperability with foreign militaries, given the increasing frequency of U.S. involvement in international coalition operations. While we agree that interoperability usually has an international connotation, we think that the term *standardized* should be limited, for Army purposes, to the definition given earlier.

---

[9]   Hybridization is possible within an organization as well as within a system (such as the IFV). For instance, joint (interservice) commands and forces are inherently hybrid.

[10]   Chobham-type armor utilizes laminated metal and ceramic materials. The original British technology has been shared with the United States and Germany, while France has developed its own version.

Another potential synonym of note is *jointness*, which is usually used in the context of relations between the U.S. military services, not between international coalition partners. Although *jointness* may be equal to *interoperability* in technical contexts, *jointness* seems to suggest attitudinal and cultural dimensions that are not necessarily suggested by *interoperability*.

Finally, we note that *interoperability* is often used in the same context as *compatibility*. Our definition includes *compatibility*, but we recommend that the term *compatibility* refer more specifically to the ability to share information among digital, IT, and communication equipment and software. For example, in a joint operation, different air defense systems from different services may be tasked with working together to protect an area from air attack. The task is easier if the different systems can exchange information.

In summary, interoperable items are able to work together (see Table 3.2). The ability to work together always has a context; that context must be specified. For instance, two weapons may be described as *interoperable* because they can process the same targeting data. They are not necessarily *common*, nor do they need to share any *components*.

Differentiated

A differentiated item is an item that is intentionally different from another. *Differentiated* implies something more than *different*. Items may be different by accident, but a differentiated item is made different with some objective in mind. *Differentiation* means to make different by alteration or modification. *Differentiation* is a term that is frequently used in the civilian literature on marketing and operations management. Differentiation is most notable when it improves performance or adds capabilities. Alterations or modifications can also simplify the design or lower production costs. Whether improving performance or capabilities or lowering costs, civilian suppliers are usually trying to differentiate their products from those supplied by their competitors in an effort to make their products more attractive to consumers. Consequently, differentiated items are often described as "specialized" or "stand-out" products. We find these terms more value laden and outcome oriented than *differentiated*.

Differentiated can also be used to suggest the creation of a different or stand-alone item by separating or dividing some part of another item. Simpkin used the phrase *hiving off* to mean the assignment of a capability to a different model of vehicle rather than accepting the trade-offs that might arise when capabilities are assigned to a single model.[11] Simpkin was thinking of tank design in particular. Turreted tanks often reflect a trade-off between the size of the main armament and the size and weight of the overall vehicle. Simpkin proposed hiving off a heavy gun to a turretless variant, while placing a lighter gun in the turreted variant (Simpkin, 1979, pp. 189, 215; 1982, pp. 26, 175–177).

We recommend that *differentiated* be defined as "altered capabilities or items" (see Table 3.2). This definition is inherently comparative. The altered capabilities or items are altered or differentiated from existing capabilities or items. *Differentiation* is an important concept, principally as a contrast to *common*.

The next chapter offers civilian light bulb, military vehicular, and infantry weapon examples of each of the nine concepts we have just defined.

---

[11] The term *hiving off* reportedly comes from the splitting of a hive of bees into two hives, one with the existing queen bee and one with a new queen bee.

CHAPTER FOUR

Examples

In this chapter, we present some examples of the nine commonality-related concepts. These examples set the scene for, and provide an exercise in, the linguistic and conceptual problems and solutions tackled by this report. In the first section, we present some introductory examples of *commonality* and its eight related concepts in the context of artificial light sources—a less complex category of examples than the later military examples. The second section presents military vehicular examples, and the third section presents infantry weapon examples.

Artificial Light Sources

Figure 4.1 shows examples of artificial lighting sources for each of the nine commonality-related concepts. We begin with *common* at the bottom of Figure 4.1. If two different types (brands or models) of flashlight (or electric, battery-powered, handheld light) are fitted with the same brand and model of light bulb, those two flashlights can be said to share a *common* type of light bulb. This light bulb would be a *common component*.

Light bulbs attach or fit into the flashlight or other type of lighting system via some sort of interface. Many flashlights accept only screw-in light bulbs that screw into an appropriately sized thread, while some lamps accept only bayonet light bulbs, whose perpendicular metal pins fit under catches in the lamp socket. Both types of interfaces can be described as *standardized*, because the design and size of the screw threads or bayonet sockets conform to the industry's standard designs. A manufacturer knows that it can design a new bulb to the interface standard and that it will connect.

If a light bulb burns out and one of the same brand and model is not available, it may be possible to replace it with a different brand or model of bulb that conforms to the same standard of socket. The new bulb would be said to be *interchangeable* with the other. The bulbs do not need to be common to be interchangeable. They could be different in shape or power and have different type designators or numbers, but they both fit into the same system and perform the same function. Their interchangeability is enabled by a standardized interface.

A portable artificial lighting system might be used with certain add-on devices or *modules*, such as an optional solar panel recharger. A *module* is a component designed to be optionally fitted to a system to change the functionality of that system; it does not have any intended stand-alone functionality. The flashlight that can be recharged by the solar recharger is part of a *modular* system. Only systems can be modular; only components can be modules.

Figure 4.1
Introductory Examples of Commonality and Eight Related Concepts

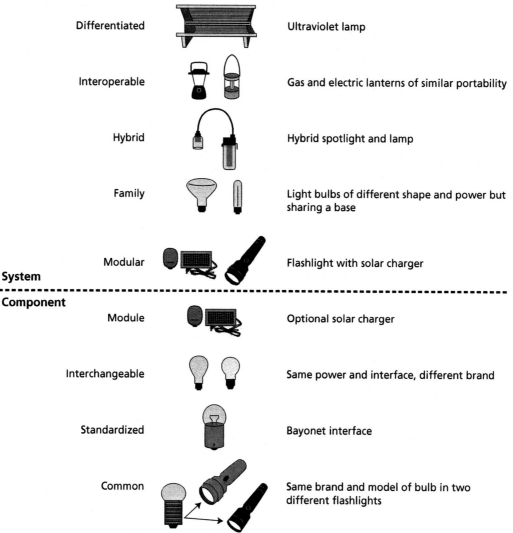

A manufacturer might produce two different models of light bulb (to offer consumers some choices in power) with the same (a common) base (the screw interface, electric contacts, and structure into which the rest of the bulb fits). Those two models of light bulb can be called *variants* within a *family* of light bulbs using a common base.

A manufacturer might create a product that has a wide-area lamp at one end and a spotlight at the other. This system is a called a *hybrid*, since it combines two different capabilities that are normally separated.

Two different manufacturers might produce different types of lamps that use different power sources (for instance, one using an electric battery, the other burning compressed butane gas). If those lamps are of similar weight and size and are fitted with similar handles, the lamps are similarly portable. They can be described as *interoperable*, at least in terms of portability. This is true even though the lamps probably do not share any components. The example of portability is chosen to distinguish interoperability from compatibility. *Compatibility* is a subset of *interoperability*. Compatible items are those that interface or communicate in some way. For instance, an electric light system might utilize a charger plugged into a car lighter or outlet. The charger and outlet would be compatible. Interoperability includes compatibility but also includes other ways in which entities can work together, such as through their similar portability.

Some systems and components are very different from others. An ultraviolet light bulb designed for use in tanning beds is a highly *differentiated* light bulb; it is clearly differentiated from a standard light bulb used in most home lamps. Its components and capabilities share little with the other systems and components already discussed. Differentiation allows a product to offer specialized capabilities and to be differentiated (in marketing terms) from competitive products.

Military Vehicular Examples

To further explain our definitions, we present military vehicular examples in this section (see Figure 4.2) and infantry weapon examples in the third section of this chapter.

As an example of a *common* item, we present a common power plant in two vehicles: the M2 Bradley IFV and the MLRS. There is an explanation for the fact that these two vehicles share a power plant: The MLRS was developed on the Bradley's chassis. Nevertheless, common power plants are rare across variants, since they are often modified or altered. In this case, the common power plant was a design requirement of the MLRS. The same power plant can be placed in either vehicle during manufacture, and the two vehicles can interchange power plants in the field.

By contrast, the M60 MBT and the M88 RV do not share a power plant, though their power plants share lower-level items. The M88 is a variant of the M60. The M60 power plant was altered to serve the M88. The power plant requires special parts and assembly to fit each vehicle and cannot be interchanged between vehicles without alteration. The power plants share the majority of components, but the power plants themselves are not entirely common. Instead, the engines are best described as *standardized*, in that they meet some of the same performance and material standards and are produced on the same production line with ease.

Some items can be manufactured by different manufacturers to different designs but can still be interchanged. Examples of such items include the Michelin XL and Goodyear AT2A pneumatic tires, which do not share the same manufacturer or tread but can be interchanged (subject to configuration restrictions) on the HEMTT.

Vehicular *modules* are difficult to code because of the ambiguity about whether a modular item is really reconfigurable or simply a base model for variants. (A vehicle's machine-gun ring mount, which can mount a different type of machine gun within a few minutes because the weapon fits an existing interface on the mounting, is part of a modular system. A vehicle that could mount that weapon but only with a specially constructed mounting is not part of a modular system but is capable of conversion into a variant.) Vehicles that can be reconfigured in the field are difficult to code, since it is difficult to know how burdensome the reconfiguration must be before we code it as a rebuild or modification. For instance, mine plows or rollers can be fitted on the front of some armored vehicles. If the modification is routinely reversed in the field, we would code the attachment as a module. If not, then the modified vehicle is a variant.

Figure 4.2
Military Vehicular Examples of the Nine Concepts

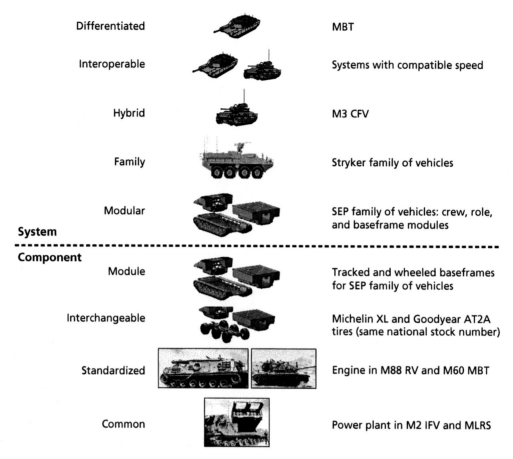

Differentiated		MBT
Interoperable		Systems with compatible speed
Hybrid		M3 CFV
Family		Stryker family of vehicles
Modular		SEP family of vehicles: crew, role, and baseframe modules

System

Component

Module		Tracked and wheeled baseframes for SEP family of vehicles
Interchangeable		Michelin XL and Goodyear AT2A tires (same national stock number)
Standardized		Engine in M88 RV and M60 MBT
Common		Power plant in M2 IFV and MLRS

NOTE: SEP = Spitterskyddad Enhets Platform.

Reconfiguration in the manufacturing plant is easier to code. One example is the SEP light armored vehicle, which was ordered by Sweden from BAE Systems Hägglunds. The manufacturer offers wheeled and tracked versions with different modular fighting compartments. The chassis and fighting compartments can be described as *modules*. The key feature of these modules (as opposed to other components that we would not code as modules) is that they change the functionality of the vehicle. The tracked or wheeled chassis changes the vehicle's mobility, while the different fighting compartments turn the variant into a heavily armed fighting vehicle, an infantry carrier, or an ambulance, among other things.

The SEP variants can be described as a *family* of vehicles, although we have indicated here that their modularity is more remarkable. The Stryker family, deployed by the U.S. Army (the first systems were delivered in February 2002), is a family of light armored vehicles. Stryker comprises two main variants—the infantry carrier vehicle (ICV) and the mobile gun system. The ICV has eight additional configurations: reconnaissance vehicle; mortar carrier; commander's vehicle; fire support vehicle; engineer squad vehicle; medical evacuation vehicle; anti-tank guided missile vehicle; and nuclear, biological, and chemical reconnaissance vehicle.

As discussed previously, the M2 Bradley IFV can be considered a variant in a family that includes the MLRS. The family also includes the M3 cavalry fighting vehicle (CFV) (as well as the Fire Support Team and Linebacker variants). The CFV was originally conceived as a hybrid vehicle, offering the armored reconnaissance capabilities of a light tank as well as the carrying capabilities of a scout-team carrier, but the CFV was too light to fight as a tank and too unstealthy to serve as a scout vehicle.

The Bradley IFV was developed to share similar mobility with the M1 Abrams MBT. In the context of mobility, it is interoperable with the M1 Abrams. In other contexts, it is not interoperable: It lacks the same level of protection or armament, even though it also carries tank-killing weapons. Consequently, although doctrine allows for the IFV to act as "overwatch" or fire support for leading tanks, it does not recommend that IFVs routinely lead tanks (Haworth, 1999; Hunnicutt, 1999).

The M1 Abrams is a highly differentiated vehicle. It is *differentiated* in capabilities, being the U.S. Army's main tank-killing ground vehicle. It has not been used as the basis for any variants, though an IFV variant was once considered (but rejected as too expensive and overly capable). It is also differentiated in components, most of which are unique to this vehicle. Its armament, protection, and engine power are unmatched by any other U.S. Army vehicle.

Infantry Weapon Examples

Figure 4.3 shows some examples of infantry weapons, categorized by each of the nine concepts. First, we note the *common* magazine, which can be fitted to the M16 rifle and M4 carbine. The magazine is one model, manufactured for both carbines.

The bayonet lugs (the fittings for the bayonet) on the two carbines meet the same *standards* for diameter, length, and other attributes, allowing the two weapons to fit the same bayonet.

The M2 and M9 bayonets are *interchangeable*. The bayonets are of different design but can be interchanged on the M4 carbine.

The optical sight is a *module*. It can be mounted on the carbine in place of the iron or vane sights. The optical sight changes the functionality of the system, allowing it to be fired more accurately, at longer ranges, or at night (depending on the type of sight used).

Since it can mount the optical sight, which is a module, the M16 rifle is inherently *modular*. Another example of the M16 rifle's modularity is that the M203 grenade launcher can be fitted underneath the rifle and later detached.

Since the M4 carbine was developed from the M16 rifle and shares many components, the M16 rifle and M4 carbine are variants in a *family* of infantry weapons.

A clear example of *hybrid* is the integral rifle/grenade launcher variant in the AK47 family of infantry weapons. The rifle and grenade launcher are combined during manufacturing and are not designed for easy reconfiguration in the field. Therefore, the system is best described as hybrid, not modular.

Infantry weapons that are similar in weight and dimensions are *interoperable* in terms of portability; each type of weapon should be able to demonstrate the same mobility and range. This is remarkable in the case of the squad automatic weapon, the M249 light machine gun, in that its weight and dimensions are closer to those of a rifle, even though its rate and sustainability of fire are closer to those of a light machine gun.

Figure 4.3
Infantry Weapon Examples of the Nine Concepts

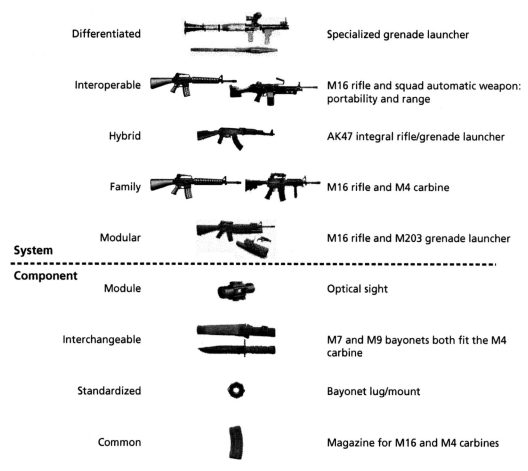

Differentiated		Specialized grenade launcher
Interoperable		M16 rifle and squad automatic weapon: portability and range
Hybrid		AK47 integral rifle/grenade launcher
Family		M16 rifle and M4 carbine
Modular		M16 rifle and M203 grenade launcher

System
- -
Component

Module		Optical sight
Interchangeable		M7 and M9 bayonets both fit the M4 carbine
Standardized		Bayonet lug/mount
Common		Magazine for M16 and M4 carbines

Finally, a traditional rocket-propelled grenade launcher is a *differentiated* weapon in that it fires heavier grenades than those fired by modules, such as the M203, and can fire only grenades, unlike the modular M16/M203.

The next chapter completes this report with some brief recommendations and conclusions.

CHAPTER FIVE

Recommendations and Conclusions

The Army, and DoD generally, is increasingly interested in acquiring "systems" that share common "components." Commonality offers many advantages and disadvantages that are sometimes difficult to discern and optimally trade off. This difficulty is compounded by semantic confusion about the subject. There is strong evidence that the existing lexicon used by the Army for *commonality* and its related concepts is ambiguous. The Army's and the U.S. military's own definitions often overlap or contain inconsistencies. Additionally, the Army, and the U.S. military generally, often fails to formally define some of the concepts identified as both relevant and important in this work.

Anecdotal evidence suggests that ambiguous terminology has led to confused discussions about the U.S. military's acquisition of new systems. Sharing a clear terminology would help designers, developers, procurers, trainers, logisticians, and operators to work together and make better decisions. Rigorous definitions help delineate problems and solutions and thus advance theory. In this case, rigorous conceptualization can help clarify the costs and benefits of different paths of action and so produce better decisions.

To achieve the goal of clarity in communication across all aspects of item procurement and life cycle, the Army should adopt a more rigorous lexicon of the sort recommended here and market it to all stakeholders. These stakeholders include Department of the Army concept developers, procurers, trainers, logisticians, and operators, and others outside of the Army: private-sector designers, developers, suppliers, and joint decisionmakers. The Army should consider using examples, such as those provided in this report, to help teach the definitions and concepts. Army procurers, developers, program executive officers, and logisticians should be directly trained in the preferred definitions and encouraged to use them in their related activities. By incorporating more consistent definitions in its formal dictionary and appropriately publicizing the definitions in its procurement, development, and logistics documents, the Army could avoid potentially costly future miscommunications. In so doing, it could achieve higher payoffs from decisions regarding future investments in commonality and families of systems.

Although readers may not agree with all our definitions, we hope that this report will serve as a sound basis for a rigorous lexicon that the Army—at least the development, procurement, and logistics communities—could adopt and utilize for the better. Future work might address how this or another rigorous lexicon could improve decisionmaking across a broad spectrum of activities related to the acquisition and maintenance of Army systems.

References

American Heritage Dictionary of the English Language, 4th ed., Boston: Houghton Mifflin, 2000. As of April 26, 2007:
http://www.bartleby.com/61/

Baldwin, Carliss Y., and Kim B. Clark, *Design Rules*, Vol. 1: *The Power of Modularity*, Cambridge, Mass.: MIT Press, 2000.

Decker, Oscar C., "The Patton Tanks: The Cold War Learning Series," in George F. Hofmann and Donn A. Starry, eds., *Camp Colt to Desert Storm: The History of U.S. Armored Forces*, Lexington, Ky.: University Press of Kentucky, 1999, pp. 298–323.

Defense Acquisition University, *Glossary of Defense Acquisition Acronyms and Terms*, 12th ed., Ft. Belvoir, Va.: Defense Acquisition University Press, July 2005. As of April 25, 2007:
http://www.dau.mil/pubs/glossary/12th_Glossary_2005.pdf

Eynan, Amit, and Meir J. Rosenblatt, "Component Commonality Effects on Inventory Costs," *Institute of Industrial Engineers Transactions*, Vol. 28, No. 2, February 1996, pp. 93–104.

Haworth, W. Blair, Jr., *The Bradley and How It Got That Way: Technology, Institutions, and the Problem of Mechanized Infantry in the United States Army*, Westport, Conn.: Greenwood Press, 1999.

Headquarters, U.S. Department of the Army, *Dictionary of United States Army Terms*, Washington, D.C., Army Regulation 310-25, October 15, 1983. As of May 8, 2007:
http://www.fas.org/irp//doddir/army/ar310-25.pdf

Headquarters, U.S. Department of the Army, U.S. Department of the Air Force, and U.S. Department of the Navy, *Technical Manual: Unit and Direct Support Maintenance Manual (Including Repair Parts and Special Tools List)*, Washington, D.C., 2001.

Hunnicutt, R. P., *Bradley: A History of American Fighting and Support Vehicles*, Novato, Calif.: Presidio, 1999.

Joint Chiefs of Staff, *Department of Defense Dictionary of Military and Associated Terms*, Washington, D.C.: U.S. Government Printing Office, Joint Publication 1-02, April 12, 2001 (as amended March 22, 2007). As of April 25, 2007:
http://www.dtic.mil/doctrine/jel/new_pubs/jp1_02.pdf

Kotov, Vadim, *Systems of Systems as Communicating Structures*, Hewlett Packard Laboratories technical report HPL-97-124, October 1997. As of April 25, 2007:
http://www.hpl.hp.com/techreports/97/HPL-97-124.html

Merriman, H. A., "Fixed Wing Aircraft," in K. Perkins, ed., *Weapons and Warfare: Conventional Weapons and Their Roles in Battle*, London: Brassey's, 1987, pp. 83–96.

Meyer, Marc H., and Alvin P. Lehnerd, *The Power of Product Platforms: Building Value and Cost Leadership*, New York: Free Press, 1997.

Nagarur, Nagen, and Abdullahil Azeem, "Impact of Commonality and Flexibility on Manufacturing Performance: A Simulation Study," *International Journal of Production Economics*, Vols. 60–61, April 1999, pp. 125–134.

Office of the Under Secretary of Defense for Acquisition, Technology, and Logistics, "'System of Systems' and 'Family of Systems' FAQs," undated fact sheet. As of April 25, 2007:
http://www.acq.osd.mil/dpap/Docs/FAQs%20--%20SoS%20&%20FoS.doc

Ogorkiewicz, Richard M., *Armoured Forces: A History of Armoured Forces and Their Vehicles*, New York: Arco, 1970.

Perera, H. S. C., Nagen Nagarur, and Mario T. Tabucanon, "Component Part Standardization: A Way to Reduce the Life-Cycle Costs of Products," *International Journal of Production Economics*, Vols. 60–61, April 1999, pp. 109–116.

Robertson, David, and Karl Ulrich, "Planning for Product Platforms," *Sloan Management Review*, Vol. 39, No. 4, Summer 1998, pp. 19–31.

Schultz, Thomas J., Associate Director, Systems Development and Production Issues, U.S. General Accounting Office, National Security and International Affairs Division, letter to C. W. Bill Young, Chairman, and John P. Murtha, Ranking Minority Member, Subcommittee on National Security, Committee on Appropriations, U.S. House of Representatives, GAO/NSAID-95-87R, February 6, 1995. As of April 25, 2007:
http://archive.gao.gov/paprpdf1/153430.pdf

Simpkin, Richard E., *Tank Warfare: An Analysis of Soviet and NATO Tank Philosophy*, London: Brassey's, 1979.

———, *Antitank: An Airmechanized Response to Armored Threats in the 90s*, Oxford: Brassey's, 1982.

Smith, Merritt Roe, ed., *Military Enterprise and Technological Change: Perspectives on the American Experience*, Cambridge, Mass.: MIT Press, 1987.

Terry, T. W., S. R. Jackson, C. E. S. Ryley, B. E. Jones, and P. J. H. Wormell, *Fighting Vehicles*, Land Warfare: Brassey's New Battlefield Weapon Systems and Technology Series, Vol. 7, London: Brassey's, 1991.

Walker, J. R., "Air-to-Surface Weapons," in K. Perkins, ed., *Weapons and Warfare: Conventional Weapons and Their Roles in Battle*, London: Brassey's, 1987, pp. 1–54.

Winchester, Jim, ed., *The Aviation Factfile: Aircraft of World War II*, San Diego, Calif.: Thunder Bay Press, 2004.